BAF

GREAT

OUTDOORS

INAPPROPRIATE

ADVICE

COLUMN

CW00395192

RALPH STORER

First published 2019

ISBN: 978-1796507126

Text, design, photographs and typesetting by Ralph Storer

No vice is so bad as advice.

Marie Dressler

Dear Reader

As the Entertainments Convenor of the Go-Take-a-Hike Mountaineering Club, I am constantly astounded by the size of my bulging postbag. The number of heartfelt letters I receive, seeking my expert advice on the most intractable personal problems, is truly humbling. When even outdoors recreation fails to provide solace, my readers know they can trust me to address their every concern with the tact and compassion it deserves. In this book, by sharing the wisdom I have gained from many years of personal pleasure in the Great Outdoors, I hope to provide reassurance to you too that, whatever your problem, it is not insoluble.

Baffies

Dear Baffies

My boyfriend loves poring over maps and planning walking routes to try to impress me, but he constantly under-estimates their length. Do you think it would help if I buy him one of those map-measuring things?

Exhausted of Exmouth

Dear Exhausted

Definitely. Then the next time he's tracing out one of his routes, tell him to take out his thing and measure it. If that doesn't impress you, dump him.

Baffies

Dear Baffies

S ince my husband and I parted, I've started going winter walking with a group of dog lovers, but my little Chihuahua often gets very cold. Do you have any suggestions as to how I can keep it warm?

Chilled of Shepherd's Bush

Dear Chilled

If your little Chihuahua is more than usually sensitive to the cold, make sure it's well wrapped up. This will also prevent the hairs becoming rimed with frost. If it tinkles when you walk, more hands-on measures may be required. For a quick rush of heat, friction is a good source of warmth. A brisk rub with an old woollen sock will provide immediate relief for the little growler. In an emergency, flagellation with a sprig of heather can prove surprisingly effective.

Baffies

Dear Baffies

I have my eye on a stylish new pair of comfortable stretch-waist outdoor trousers that perfectly compliment my navy blue check shirt. Among other useful features, they have a zipped pocket that's the perfect size for my multi-function pen-knife, which features scissors, tweezers, a can opener and a fire-starting flint as well as a knife. My only problem is which colour to purchase: beige or lovat green. Can you advise?

Discriminating of Doddington

Dear Discriminating

I recommend beige. It suits your personality.

Baffies

Dear Baffies

I enjoy a gentle hill walk but my wife prefers a stiff one. How can we find something to satisfy both of us?

Befuddled of Boghall

Dear Befuddled

For goodness sake, take her up somewhere that'll bring some colour to her cheeks.

Baffies

Dear Baffies

Over the decades I have suffered grievously at the hands of the Press and am writing to you in the hope that you can restore my reputation. I am simply an innocent victim of lurid travellers' tales. It was these that forced me into the wilds in the first place. I cannot help how I look and there's surely no place today for the continued prejudice against me. My equally maligned colleague Nessie has similar issues. We are not monsters.

*The Big Grey Man
of Ben Macdui*

Dear Big Man

I'm happy to print your letter and assist in your rehabilitation. I have to say, though, that you're your own worst enemy. If you insist on looming out of the mist with a blood-curdling wail you're never going to create a favourable first impression. You also continue to conceal the exact location of your domicile. Why not open it up as a tourist attraction and let visitors see the real you? P.S. If Nessie would like to write in confidence, I'd be happy to reply in kind

Baffies

Dear Baffies

While out walking with my wife recently, I broke the thumb of my right hand when I tripped and twisted it in the wrist loop of my walking pole. The plaster cast is off, but I'm still unable to grip my pole to any benefit. My left hand is useless for the job, so what should I do?

Thumbless of Trumpton

Dear Thumbless

Wrist loops are death traps. You're lucky you only broke your thumb. Until your right hand recovers I suggest you leave your pole alone for a while and ask your wife to lend you a hand when necessary.

Baffies

Dear Baffies

I have purchased a mountain bike and am more than pleased with the way long walk-ins have become shorter ride-ins. However, the constant pounding on rutted forest tracks leaves me so sore at the end of the day that I can barely walk straight. Can you suggest a remedy?

Sore Susan of Stoke Poges

Dear Sore Susan

I have little experience in your area, but a female friend tells me she used to suffer from the same problem until she discovered the Easy Rider saddle, which is specially designed with the female anatomy in mind to heighten the riding experience. She says that descending a bumpy forest track can leave her quite red-faced, but this is surely a small price to pay for a more pleasurable experience.

Baffies

Dear Baffies

I'm having difficulty pitching my new wigwam tent. I've never had erection problems before but it's a fiddle even getting the thing out of its carry-bag. I can't even get the centre pole to stand upright long enough to find enough guys to hold it steady. Not only that but, once up and despite being firmly pegged at the base, it flops from side to side in the slightest breeze. To cap it all, the zipper on the fly keeps snagging and once even drew blood from my pinkie. Am I doing something wrong?

Wiggy of Wigglesworth

Dear Wiggy

Y ou'll be relieved to hear that this is not an uncommon problem. If you can't manage to get it up on your own I suggest you seek help. There are usually a few guys hanging around the campsite toilet block who'll be more than happy to lend a hand.

Baffies

Dear Baffies

Please, please, please tell me how I can keep midges away when camping in the Scottish Highlands. You are my last resort. If you can't help me I fear I may end up jumping in the nearest loch.

Had It Up To Here
of Hull

Dear Had It Up To Here

Invest in some lead weights to keep you down. That's the only solution.

Baffies

Dear Baffies

I'm writing to you in confidence about a delicate problem I have concerning my girlfriend's new hiking shorts. They're so tight that I can't concentrate and find myself stumbling along in her wake, breathing more heavily than is good for me. What can I do?

Puffed Out of Strathpeffer

Dear Puffed Out

Get fitter so you can hold your own.

Baffies

Dear Baffies

My two sons, aged 12 and 10, used to be nice boys but now they recoil at the very idea of going hillwalking with me. The younger has taken to lying on his stomach and beating the ground with his fists, while the elder goes into sulk mode and refuses to speak. How can I force them to enjoy our outings?

Harassed of Hockwold cum Wilton

Dear Harassed

Children are vile creatures that are best incarcerated in some kind of holding cell pending your return. If they must accompany you, a promise of sweets later may give a temporary reprieve from whining. If you exhaust them sufficiently, they may even forget the promise so you won't have to cough up. As a last resort use the carrot and stick method to keep the brats in check. A vacuum flask can substitute for a carrot and a walking pole makes a useful stick. Beat them with both.

Baffies

Dear Baffies

I've been teaching my girlfriend to rock climb but now she's got the hang of it she wants to try something longer and harder than I can manage. What should I do?

Crestfallen of Littlehampton

Dear Crestfallen

You've only got yourself to blame, pal. If you can't deal with your girlfriend's new-found passion you shouldn't have taken her up in the first place. Now she's got a taste for it she naturally wants someone who can offer her something a tad more exhilarating than she can get from a scree-for-brains such as yourself.

Baffies

Dear Baffies

My wife and I have just returned from a weekend in Glen Coe, where we made a traverse of the Aonach Eagach ridge. I thought she'd love it, but she got scared and blamed me. Now she won't even talk to me. Isn't she being unreasonable?

Perplexed of Pitlochry

Dear Perplexed

Listen very carefully. A woman is never being unreasonable. The fault is entirely yours. Your only recourse is begging. As much as is required.

Baffies

Dear Baffies

While scrambling in the Cuillin I slipped and scraped my shin on an extrusion of rough gabbro, which has left me with an unsightly scar. I used to wear shorts but now I have to wear long trousers even in the height of summer. Is there any way round this?

Embarrassed of Ecclefechan

Dear Embarrassed

Stop being such a namby-pamby. A Cuillin scar is a badge of honour to be treasured. Attract admiring glances by wearing shorts at all times. This is especially important in the depths of winter, when the scar should show up nicely against pale skin.

Baffies

Dear Baffies

When my boyfriend and I go camping he always makes a mess in the vestibule. I like to keep it neat and tidy, which allows more room for manoeuvre and easier access to the interior. He doesn't mind a bit of clambering to get in, but I prefer to keep everything in good order. How can I get him to treat the area with respect?

Shipshape of Bristol

Dear Shipshape

You'll be pleased to hear that there's a tried and tested solution to this problem that has never been known to fail: refuse him entrance until he mends his ways.

Baffies

Dear Baffies

I've purchased one of those new-fangled pop-up tents. Self-erection is a marvellous step forward, but the thing tends to pop up in the most inappropriate situations. Last weekend I was camping on a riverbank with my girlfriend. When she bent over to rummage in her fanny pack the thing popped up unexpectedly and nearly turfed her into the water. It was a devil of a problem to get it back down again. What's your view on pop-ups?

*Hard Up of
Hampton Wick*

Dear Hard Up

Pop-ups are fine in theory but unmanageable in practice unless treated with a firm hand. To avoid an inappropriate erection, make sure your pop-up is kept tightly under wraps when it's not needed. Once up, folding it away again is, as you have discovered, an acquired skill whose success depends on the correct wrist action. The best way to resolve these technical issues is repeated practice with your girlfriend.

Baffies

Dear Baffies

My climbing instructor is too yummy for words. When he straps me into my harness at the foot of the climbing wall I nearly faint. How can I show him I'm interested?

Eager Beaver of Berwick

Dear Eager Beaver

You really have led a sheltered life, haven't you? If you can't get his hands to wander while he's tying you in, it's time you took some yoga classes and learnt some new positions. If that still doesn't do the trick, try fiddling with his bowline.

Baffies

Dear Baffies

I'm worried about my husband, who isn't getting any younger. He still goes winter hillwalking with an old wooden ice axe whose shaft he lovingly lubricates with linseed oil before use. He says this increases its rigidity and longevity. I tell him to swap it for a newer model, but he says it has served him well in many tight spots. He seems happy to persevere with it even though the shaft is now so gnarled and greasy that his hand keeps falling off the end.

Worried of West Wittering

Dear Worried

As long as your husband's equipment continues to serve him well, I wouldn't worry. I suspect you'd prefer him to put it away for the winter, but would that really give either of you any satisfaction? Look at it this way: as long as he continues to lubricate the shaft there'll never be a problem with splinters.

Baffies

Dear Baffies

I seek your advice on a delicate matter of etiquette. While nearing the summit of Helvellyn recently, I saw a woman approaching from the far side, apparently totally naked apart from a pair of boots. Being a gentleman and not wishing to cause her embarrassment, I gave her a wide berth. However, what should I do if such an encounter were to occur on a narrow ridge such as Striding Edge?

Gentleman Jim

Dear Gentleman Jim

You have two options: block her passage or toss yourself off. A gentleman would do the latter.

Baffies

Dear Baffies

I love backpacking with my partner, especially intimate nights in the wild in our cosy little geodesic. The only downside is his beard. He shaves before we leave but after a few days I feel my face is being exfoliated by a cheese grater. Do you have any remedies?

Ground Down of Grimsby

Dear Ground Down

Wear one of those skier's face masks with holes for eyes and nose. Not only will this mitigate against wear and tear but, if you're as adventurous as your letter suggests, it may add a new dimension to your relationship. If this should cause him to stray to other delicate areas a useful safe word is the German for motorway exit: 'Ausfahrt' .

Baffies

Dear Baffies

I am in a quandary. I find myself having to choose between two attractive boyfriends. One of them is a better partner on the hill — he even carries my water bottle. The other is superior when it comes to, ahem, indoor sports. As someone who enjoys both pursuits, I can't bear to forsake either, so which one should I choose?

Confused of Cockermouth

44

Dear Confused

As your two favourite pursuits are more or less mutually exclusive, why not interleave your two admirers? Failing that, for the best of both worlds, dump both of them and give me a call.

Baffies

Dear Baffies

I wish to impress a young lady who I'm told likes to bag Munros. What are Munros, where can I obtain them and how big a bag do I need to put them in?

Name withheld

Dear Ignoramus

A bag big enough to go over your head should do the job. Try it. It can only increase your sexual magnetism.

Baffies

Dear Baffies

This summer I went on a climbing course in the Swiss Alps and my instructor and I fell head over heels for each other. Pierre's English wasn't great but we didn't need words. We were happy just to romp in the edelweiss in the shadow of the Rothorn. And when he did rope me up, I was able to reach heights I'd never dreamt of. We swapped phone numbers and email addresses, but a month has passed and he hasn't been in touch. What should I do?

Pining of Puckeridge

Dear Pining

Wise up, dear. Pierre's already forgotten about you and cherry-picked from his next batch of impressionable clients. Move on. If it's his length of Kernmantle you miss, I'm sure you could easily find someone in a mountaineering club who'd be happy to show you the ropes.

Baffies

Dear Baffies

I enjoy the peace and quiet of the countryside, but when my wife accompanies me for a walk she insists on sharing. She shares constantly about the weather, the view, the flowers... How can I explain to her that I prefer to commune with nature in silence?

Lone Wolf of Lowestoft

Dear Lone Wolf

Be strong. Zip your mouth shut. Pretend she's not there. Suppress all emotion. You're a man, aren't you?

Baffies

Dear Baffies

Some time ago I suffered an awkward fall from which I am now fully recovered but which has left me with no teeth. I have worn a dental plate ever since but I want to go camping with my new boyfriend and I'm scared he'll find out. Should I just try to keep my mouth shut?

Gummy Girl

52

Dear Gummy Girl

On the contrary, give him the widest toothless grin you can muster. The more he realises the possibilities, the keener he's going to be.

Baffies

Dear Baffies

My husband has taken to spending weekends in remote bothies with a mixed hillwalking group. Last week he returned with his underpants on inside out. He explained that dressing can be awkward in a cramped space with no artificial light, but I do worry for him. Is there anything you can suggest to save him from possible future embarrassment?

Concerned of Cockfosters

Dear Concerned

Y ou need to sit down and have a good think about this. Once you've figured it out, and depending on your disposition, either join him for bothy frolics or dump him.

Baffies

Dear Baffies

My wife and I are thinking of pitching our tent on a remote Cornish beach, but she's concerned that sand will get everywhere. How can I reassure her?

Shore Thing of Shrewsbury

Dear Shore Thing

There should be no problem as long as you're careful. Make sure no sand gets beyond the entrance, otherwise a stiff brush will be required to wheech it out of every nook and cranny. And always take your boots off before you enter, which is the polite thing to do anyway.

Baffies

Dear Baffies

I take my girlfriend rock climbing and have my heart set on leading her up a particularly fine line whose crux move involves a stretch across a steep rib. I can do it when I'm on my own but when I'm with her I can't get my leg over no matter how hard I try. Can you help?

Straddler of Needham

Dear Straddler

Y ou're trying too hard to impress her and this is leading to performance anxiety. Relax, shake the tension out of your body, make your move smoothly and decisively and you'll find that it comes more easily than expected.

Baffies

Dear Baffies

Since falling off Ben Nevis a few weeks ago I think I might be dead. Is this normal?

Perturbed of Pandy Tudur

Dear Perturbed

I'm happy to assuage your concerns. Being dead after falling off Ben Nevis is entirely normal. In fact I offer my congratulations. Many of my heroes are dead.

Baffies

Dear Baffies

I find the advice you dole out to be in the worst possible taste. You are rude, immoral and patronising. Please stop.

Name withheld

To Whom It May Concern

OKAY.

Baffies

SOME OF RALPH'S OTHER BOOKS

THE ULTIMATE GUIDE TO THE MUNROS series

One of the definitive guides to the Munros. PRESS AND JOURNAL

BAFFIES' EASY MUNRO GUIDE Series

A truly outstanding guidebook. UNDISCOVERED SCOTLAND

BAFFIES' GREAT OUTDOORS INAPPROPRIATE GLOSSARY

THE ULTIMATE SEX TRIVIA QUIZ BOOK

The Joy of Hillwalking
50 Shades of Hillwalking
See You on the Hill
The Ultimate Mountain Trivia Quiz Challenge
50 Best Routes on Skye and Raasay

Printed in Great Britain
by Amazon

85201289R00037